THIS NOTEBOOK
BELONGS TO:

Name

Address

Email

Phone Number

Mileage Log Book

| Model/Make: |
| Year: |

	ODOMETER				
Date	**Start**	**End**	**Total**	**Destination**	**Notes**

Mileage Log Book

Model/Make:

Year:

ODOMETER

Date	Start	End	Total	Destination	Notes

Mileage Log Book

Model/Make:

Year:

	ODOMETER				
Date	**Start**	**End**	**Total**	**Destination**	**Notes**

Mileage Log Book

Model/Make:

Year:

ODOMETER

Date	Start	End	Total	Destination	Notes

Mileage Log Book

Model/Make:

Year:

ODOMETER

Date	Start	End	Total	Destination	Notes

Mileage Log Book

Model/Make:

Year:

	ODOMETER				
Date	**Start**	**End**	**Total**	**Destination**	**Notes**

Mileage Log Book

Model/Make:

Year:

ODOMETER

Date	Start	End	Total	Destination	Notes

Mileage Log Book

Model/Make:

Year:

ODOMETER

Date	Start	End	Total	Destination	Notes

Mileage Log Book

Model/Make:

Year:

ODOMETER

Date	Start	End	Total	Destination	Notes

Mileage Log Book

Model/Make:

Year:

ODOMETER					
Date	Start	End	Total	Destination	Notes

Mileage Log Book

Model/Make:

Year:

ODOMETER					
Date	Start	End	Total	Destination	Notes

Mileage Log Book

Model/Make:

Year:

ODOMETER

Date	Start	End	Total	Destination	Notes

Mileage Log Book

Model/Make:

Year:

	ODOMETER				
Date	**Start**	**End**	**Total**	**Destination**	**Notes**

Mileage Log Book

Model/Make:

Year:

ODOMETER

Date	Start	End	Total	Destination	Notes

Mileage Log Book

Mileage Log Book

Model/Make:

Year:

ODOMETER

Date	Start	End	Total	Destination	Notes

Mileage Log Book

Model/Make:

Year:

ODOMETER

Date	Start	End	Total	Destination	Notes

Mileage Log Book

Mileage Log Book

Model/Make:

Year:

ODOMETER

Date	Start	End	Total	Destination	Notes

Mileage Log Book

Model/Make:

Year:

ODOMETER

Date	Start	End	Total	Destination	Notes

Mileage Log Book

Model/Make:

Year:

ODOMETER

Date	Start	End	Total	Destination	Notes

Mileage Log Book

Model/Make:

Year:

Date	Start	End	Total	Destination	Notes
		ODOMETER			

Mileage Log Book

Model/Make:

Year:

ODOMETER

Date	Start	End	Total	Destination	Notes

Mileage Log Book

Model/Make:

Year:

ODOMETER

Date	Start	End	Total	Destination	Notes

Mileage Log Book

Mileage Log Book

Model/Make:

Year:

ODOMETER

Date	Start	End	Total	Destination	Notes

Mileage Log Book

Model/Make:

Year:

	ODOMETER				
Date	Start	End	Total	Destination	Notes

Mileage Log Book

Model/Make:

Year:

ODOMETER

Date	Start	End	Total	Destination	Notes

Mileage Log Book

Model/Make:

Year:

ODOMETER

Date	Start	End	Total	Destination	Notes

Mileage Log Book

Model/Make:

Year:

ODOMETER

Date	Start	End	Total	Destination	Notes

Mileage Log Book

Model/Make:

Year:

| | ODOMETER | | | | |
Date	Start	End	Total	Destination	Notes

Mileage Log Book

Model/Make:

Year:

ODOMETER

Date	Start	End	Total	Destination	Notes

Mileage Log Book

Model/Make:

Year:

ODOMETER

Date	Start	End	Total	Destination	Notes

Mileage Log Book

Model/Make:

Year:

ODOMETER

Date	Start	End	Total	Destination	Notes

Mileage Log Book

Model/Make:

Year:

ODOMETER

Date	Start	End	Total	Destination	Notes

Mileage Log Book

Model/Make:

Year:

ODOMETER

Date	Start	End	Total	Destination	Notes

Mileage Log Book

Model/Make:

Year:

ODOMETER

Date	Start	End	Total	Destination	Notes

Mileage Log Book

Model/Make:

Year:

ODOMETER

Date	Start	End	Total	Destination	Notes

Mileage Log Book

Model/Make:

Year:

ODOMETER

Date	Start	End	Total	Destination	Notes

Mileage Log Book

Model/Make:

Year:

ODOMETER

Date	Start	End	Total	Destination	Notes

Mileage Log Book

Model/Make:

Year:

ODOMETER

Date	Start	End	Total	Destination	Notes

Mileage Log Book

Model/Make:

Year:

	ODOMETER				
Date	**Start**	**End**	**Total**	**Destination**	**Notes**

Mileage Log Book

Model/Make:

Year:

ODOMETER					
Date	**Start**	**End**	**Total**	**Destination**	**Notes**

Mileage Log Book

Mileage Log Book

Model/Make:

Year:

ODOMETER

Date	Start	End	Total	Destination	Notes

Mileage Log Book

| Model/Make: |
| Year: |

ODOMETER

Date	Start	End	Total	Destination	Notes

Mileage Log Book

Model/Make:

Year:

ODOMETER

Date	Start	End	Total	Destination	Notes

Mileage Log Book

Model/Make:

Year:

ODOMETER

Date	Start	End	Total	Destination	Notes

Mileage Log Book

Model/Make:

Year:

ODOMETER

Date	Start	End	Total	Destination	Notes

Mileage Log Book

Model/Make:

Year:

ODOMETER

Date	Start	End	Total	Destination	Notes

Mileage Log Book

Model/Make:

Year:

Date	ODOMETER			Destination	Notes
	Start	End	Total		

Mileage Log Book

Model/Make:

Year:

ODOMETER

Date	Start	End	Total	Destination	Notes

Mileage Log Book

Model/Make:

Year:

ODOMETER

Date	Start	End	Total	Destination	Notes

Mileage Log Book

Model/Make:

Year:

ODOMETER

Date	Start	End	Total	Destination	Notes

Mileage Log Book

Model/Make:

Year:

ODOMETER

Date	Start	End	Total	Destination	Notes

Mileage Log Book

Model/Make:

Year:

ODOMETER

Date	Start	End	Total	Destination	Notes

Mileage Log Book

Model/Make:

Year:

	ODOMETER				
Date	**Start**	**End**	**Total**	**Destination**	**Notes**

Mileage Log Book

Model/Make:

Year:

ODOMETER

Date	Start	End	Total	Destination	Notes

Mileage Log Book

Model/Make:

Year:

ODOMETER

Date	Start	End	Total	Destination	Notes

Mileage Log Book

Model/Make:

Year:

	ODOMETER				
Date	**Start**	**End**	**Total**	**Destination**	**Notes**

Mileage Log Book

Model/Make:

Year:

ODOMETER

Date	Start	End	Total	Destination	Notes

Mileage Log Book

Model/Make:

Year:

ODOMETER

Date	Start	End	Total	Destination	Notes

Mileage Log Book

Model/Make:

Year:

	ODOMETER				
Date	Start	End	Total	Destination	Notes

Mileage Log Book

Model/Make:

Year:

ODOMETER

Date	Start	End	Total	Destination	Notes

Mileage Log Book

Model/Make:

Year:

ODOMETER

Date	Start	End	Total	Destination	Notes

Mileage Log Book

Model/Make:

Year:

ODOMETER

Date	Start	End	Total	Destination	Notes

Mileage Log Book

Model/Make:

Year:

ODOMETER

Date	Start	End	Total	Destination	Notes

Mileage Log Book

Model/Make:

Year:

ODOMETER

Date	Start	End	Total	Destination	Notes

Mileage Log Book

Model/Make:

Year:

ODOMETER

Date	Start	End	Total	Destination	Notes

Mileage Log Book

Model/Make:
Year:

ODOMETER

Date	Start	End	Total	Destination	Notes

Mileage Log Book

Mileage Log Book

Model/Make:

Year:

ODOMETER

Date	Start	End	Total	Destination	Notes

Mileage Log Book

Model/Make:

Mileage Log Book

Model/Make:

Year:

	ODOMETER				
Date	**Start**	**End**	**Total**	**Destination**	**Notes**

Mileage Log Book

Model/Make:

Year:

ODOMETER

Date	Start	End	Total	Destination	Notes

Mileage Log Book

Model/Make:

Year:

ODOMETER

Date	Start	End	Total	Destination	Notes

Mileage Log Book

Mileage Log Book

Model/Make:

Year:

ODOMETER

Date	Start	End	Total	Destination	Notes

Mileage Log Book

Model/Make:

Year:

	ODOMETER				
Date	**Start**	**End**	**Total**	**Destination**	**Notes**

Mileage Log Book

Mileage Log Book

Model/Make:

Year:

ODOMETER

Date	Start	End	Total	Destination	Notes

Mileage Log Book

Model/Make:

Year:

	ODOMETER				
Date	**Start**	**End**	**Total**	**Destination**	**Notes**

Mileage Log Book

Model/Make:

Year:

ODOMETER

Date	Start	End	Total	Destination	Notes

Mileage Log Book

Model/Make:

Year:

ODOMETER

Date	Start	End	Total	Destination	Notes

Mileage Log Book

Model/Make:

Year:

ODOMETER

Date	Start	End	Total	Destination	Notes

Mileage Log Book

Model/Make:

Year:

ODOMETER

Date	Start	End	Total	Destination	Notes

Mileage Log Book

Mileage Log Book

| Model/Make: |
| Year: |

ODOMETER

Date	Start	End	Total	Destination	Notes

Mileage Log Book

Model/Make:

Year:

ODOMETER

Date	Start	End	Total	Destination	Notes

Mileage Log Book

Model/Make:

Year:

ODOMETER

Date	Start	End	Total	Destination	Notes

Mileage Log Book

Model/Make:

Year:

	ODOMETER				
Date	**Start**	**End**	**Total**	**Destination**	**Notes**

Mileage Log Book   **Model/Make:**

Mileage Log Book

Model/Make:

Year:

ODOMETER

Date	Start	End	Total	Destination	Notes

Mileage Log Book

Model/Make:

Year:

ODOMETER

Date	Start	End	Total	Destination	Notes

Mileage Log Book

Model/Make:

Year:

		ODOMETER			
Date	**Start**	**End**	**Total**	**Destination**	**Notes**

Mileage Log Book

Model/Make:
Year:

ODOMETER

Date	Start	End	Total	Destination	Notes

Mileage Log Book

Model/Make:

Year:

ODOMETER

Date	Start	End	Total	Destination	Notes

Mileage Log Book

Model/Make:

Year:

	ODOMETER				
Date	**Start**	**End**	**Total**	**Destination**	**Notes**

Mileage Log Book

Model/Make:

Year:

ODOMETER

Date	Start	End	Total	Destination	Notes

Mileage Log Book

Model/Make:

Year:

	ODOMETER				
Date	**Start**	**End**	**Total**	**Destination**	**Notes**

Mileage Log Book

Model/Make:

Year:

ODOMETER

Date	Start	End	Total	Destination	Notes

Mileage Log Book

Model/Make:

Year:

ODOMETER

Date	Start	End	Total	Destination	Notes

Mileage Log Book

Model/Make:

Year:

ODOMETER

Date	Start	End	Total	Destination	Notes

Mileage Log Book

Model/Make:

Year:

ODOMETER

Date	Start	End	Total	Destination	Notes

Mileage Log Book   Model/Make:

Mileage Log Book

Model/Make:

Year:

ODOMETER

Date	Start	End	Total	Destination	Notes

Mileage Log Book

Model/Make:

Year:

ODOMETER

Date	Start	End	Total	Destination	Notes

Mileage Log Book

Model/Make:

Year:

ODOMETER

Date	Start	End	Total	Destination	Notes

Mileage Log Book

Model/Make:

Year:

ODOMETER

Date	Start	End	Total	Destination	Notes

Mileage Log Book

Model/Make:

Year:

Date	Start	End	Total	Destination	Notes
		ODOMETER			

Mileage Log Book

Model/Make:

Year:

ODOMETER

Date	Start	End	Total	Destination	Notes

Mileage Log Book

Model/Make:

Year:

ODOMETER

Date	Start	End	Total	Destination	Notes

Mileage Log Book

Model/Make:

Year:

ODOMETER

Date	Start	End	Total	Destination	Notes

Mileage Log Book

Model/Make:

Year:

ODOMETER

Date	Start	End	Total	Destination	Notes

Mileage Log Book

Model/Make:

Year:

ODOMETER

Date	Start	End	Total	Destination	Notes

Mileage Log Book

Model/Make:

Year:

ODOMETER

Date	Start	End	Total	Destination	Notes

Mileage Log Book

Model/Make:

Year:

ODOMETER

Date	Start	End	Total	Destination	Notes

Mileage Log Book   Model/Make:

Mileage Log Book

Model/Make:

Year:

ODOMETER

Date	Start	End	Total	Destination	Notes

Mileage Log Book

Model/Make:

Year:

ODOMETER

Date	Start	End	Total	Destination	Notes

Mileage Log Book

Model/Make:

Year:

ODOMETER

Date	Start	End	Total	Destination	Notes

Mileage Log Book

Model/Make:

Year:

ODOMETER

Date	Start	End	Total	Destination	Notes

Mileage Log Book

Mileage Log Book

Model/Make:

Year:

ODOMETER

Date	Start	End	Total	Destination	Notes

Mileage Log Book

Model/Make:

Year:

	ODOMETER				
Date	**Start**	**End**	**Total**	**Destination**	**Notes**

Mileage Log Book **Model/Make:**

Mileage Log Book

Model/Make:

Year:

ODOMETER

Date	Start	End	Total	Destination	Notes

Mileage Log Book

Model/Make:

Year:

ODOMETER

Date	Start	End	Total	Destination	Notes

Mileage Log Book

Model/Make:

Year:

ODOMETER

Date	Start	End	Total	Destination	Notes

Mileage Log Book

Model/Make:

Year:

| | ODOMETER | | | | |
Date	Start	End	Total	Destination	Notes

Mileage Log Book

Mileage Log Book

Model/Make:

Year:

ODOMETER

Date	Start	End	Total	Destination	Notes

Mileage Log Book

Model/Make:

Year:

ODOMETER

Date	Start	End	Total	Destination	Notes

Mileage Log Book   Model/Make: